Yello

THOMAS A. CLARK lives in a si
of Scotland. His publications inc
cations, 2005), *The Hundred Th* ...... (Carcanet, 2008), and
numerous small books and cards from his own Moschatel Press. In
the summer months, with the artist Laurie Clark, he runs Cairn, a
project space for new art (www.cairneditions.blogspot.com). In
exploration of some formal possibilities of poetry, Thomas A.
Clark's work often appears as installations or interventions in
galleries or in domestic or public spaces.

THOMAS A. CLARK

Yellow & Blue

CARCANET

First published in Great Britain in 2014 by
Carcanet Press Limited
Alliance House
Cross Street
Manchester M2 7AQ

www.carcanet.co.uk

A CIP catalogue record for this book is available from the British Library

ISBN 978 1 84777 205 3

The publisher acknowledges financial assistance from Arts Council England

Typeset by XL Publishing Services, Exmouth
Printed and bound in England by SRP Ltd, Exeter

Yellow & Blue

on a morning early
when no one
is around
the scree slope
tumbles into
the green lochan

it happens
casually
in the light
available
on a path
that leads
away from it

the truthful ones
the sea-rocks
the skerries
rise from rough waters
into veracity
breaker of boats

skerry of the sea-bent
skerry of the dulse
the yellow skerry
skerry of the strife
to name the rocks
is to navigate
successfully among them
the sparkling skerries
skerry of the anchor
skerry of the deer
landing place of the swan

a tantrum or gale
threw rocks at the gable
tore out the garden
that sat above the sea
in lovely ferocity
poured over breakwaters
piled up plastic
against the blue door

it is a new place
this morning strange
in a light that knows
nothing of the old place
that stood intact
on a bright morning
before the storm

on rocks by the shore
a sheepdog is barking
to round up the waves
but the silly waves
break

speed of the running wave
composure of the standing wave
wit of the rippling wave
delight of the breaking wave

in a wilderness
or bewilderment
of sandwort
and bladder-wrack
small shell place
sheltered

lying back
in the marram grass
out of the wind
listening to the wind
one degree of separation
delivers the sound

there is nowhere to go
there is nothing to do
what would it be
to go somewhere
to do something
who would it be

cumulus nimbus stratus
sandstone basalt granite

it appears the moment
it is mentioned
the hill of bog-cotton
appears and disappears

the residue
of the dissolution
of being
together
huddles
in desolation
by a lonely shore

anything added
may be subtracted
forms half remembered
drift and snag
on jagged
truncated forms
quickly redescribed

when clouds lift
from misty poetry
to see
is to be enlarged
by a faculty

the peeling
birch bark
has a radiant
fringe of light

kitchen midden refuse
ashes bones limpet shells
fragments of pottery
a bit of pumice
a nodule of flint
the hilt with crossguard
of a much-corroded sword

on the cliff edge
the remnant of a net
has blown to cling
to a teasel head
torn blue windflower

flowering gorse bush
leaning over
towards the sea
as if its growth
were towards completion
of yellow in blue

as leaves have grown
back on branches
songs have come
among the leaves
a gathering
in the young
whitebeam

when one thing is tied
loosely to another
the rope drips
dew and sea water
the blue rope
dips in water
then tightens

everything
seems full
until need
fills it

an island across a strand
unapproachable approachable
unapproachable

an island defended by a wall
long ago breached by
ragwort and mountain ash

an island washed away
its lambs at pasture
under the sea

vision leads the mind
beyond islands to a light
or supplement of possibility

some negative features
cut into glacial till
reveal structural elements
a hearth and post holes
a rammed stone floor
extending to a wall
of neatly laid courses
by a threshold stone

sheep and cattle and pigs and goats
saithe and cod and crabs and hens
oats and flax and chert and flint
wood and bone and stone and iron

the vague line of a wall
may be no more than
a fortuitous arrangement
of broken stones
but where it has disappeared
a wall should be inferred
the fort of stillness
continually remade

from speed and noise
a strategic withdrawal
from conformity and self-interest
an abstention
from conspicuous consumption
an absolute retreat

against change it defends itself
against difference it defends itself
against trust it defends itself
against peace it defends itself
against doubt it defends itself

centuries of rain
onslaughts of heat and cold
loosened the structure
loss of authority
the need to stand unguarded
brought it down

in stillness the hills
bulabhal chaipabhal
bolabhal bleabhal
are resting bells
then a wind blows
chaipabhal bolabhal
bulabhal bleabhal
through the syllables

in a high slow turning of gulls
gliding and hanging
dropping and rising
joy samples its levels

the news is news
at the bus stop
in the rain
it is always the same
distant wars
the cleared land
forgotten

the morning bleak
a line of moles
hung on a wire
the burn swollen
bones picked clean

their faces are red
not from shame
but from the wind
from exposure
to their own
waywardness
big red men
striding in an innocence
regained

they go along streets
through doors
into company
airs about them
bare faced

he fell to the floor
people say
but the floor is a ground
not constructed
but given
unconditionally

drinking and falling
down on the earth
getting up and drinking
drinking and falling
down on the earth
getting up and drinking

what excuse to arrive
at an age and feel
preliminary
still raw
the tired strategies
of no avail
only error allowing
access to the real

there are flowers
in the window
of the house collapsing
into the sea
blue flowers

it is fitting to stand
longest by graves
marked only with
an uncarved stone
inserted roughly
into the earth
on a mound of grass
surrounded by a harvest
of gold by the sea

father brother friend
loving husband
wife of the above
relations set in stone
a man and his daughters
a mother and her sons
ragwort round them
the sea near them
grass over them

roots of silverweed
leaves of nettles
fear of eviction

it looks as if the ragwort
grew up in response
to a splash of yellow paint
on a fence post

some quite ordinary
but necessary thing
sunlight or kindness
or the need to be known
recognised in its absence

as if all momentum
came to resolution
hills run to the sea
green sits beside blue
today it might be true
in a light that holds it
steady for inspection

the green by the blue
the blue by the green
keep their values
as keenly as if
the green for the blue
the blue for the green

boys and girls go barefoot
over the machair
through the bentgrass
through the barley
run barefoot everywhere
daylight leads them
in clover in pursuit

in an old inequality
tenacity
of the weed in the soil
fragility
of the crop in the soil

lovely the wave
through the standing barley
a friend of pleasure
would linger
at its edge

a plane of consistency
evenly unfolding
is broken up
by brightness into
bright occasions
that dance a jig
the reel with the burl
the work of the weavers
the morning dew

brightness scatters
any assurance
of being there
there is no
where to place
the increments

something chanced on
a diversion or treasure
that the eye lights on
thought delights in
having form and colour
weight and texture
a word or wonder

in support of
on the side of
in the direction of
an inclination
in italic
for

through clay, sand and gravel
deposited by ice
as glacial drift
acid and impermeable
old peat roads lead
to bogs of sphagnum
cottongrass and deergrass
cloudberry and crowberry

on the open hill
in granite debris
are crystals
of feldspar and mica
the word gems
blue topaz
green beryl
smoky quartz

veins in gneiss
vitreous or resinous
grow geodes
or prismatic crystals
translucent yellow
hard yet ductile
of good cleavage
irregular fracture
almost always
fluorescent

a bed of calcareous rock
drilled blasted screened washed
is transported by water
to aid in the manufacture
of silicon carbide abrasives
leaving an open scar

a deserted or solitary place
desert or inner poverty
emptiness with a clump of grass
an unacres
mere lateral spread or tract

anything that arrives
interrupts a waiting
for the collapse
of expectation
it all starts up again

an insult
hurled in the face
a pebble-dash
of raindrops

on the flushed grassland
cushions of moss campion
green cyphel flowers
white alpine mouse-ear
on the slopes of corries
saxifrage and mountain pansy
take constant nourishment
from soil movement
silting of mountain rills

call it a moor
where thought is under
constant scrutiny
the view from nowhere
a brightness bristling
with thistles

under bird paths
paths of desire
take advantage of
old coffin paths
to rest by cairns
on their way down
to paths across
a mercantile sea

the spirit learns vagueness
from cloud and wool
its density loosening
clinging to wire
twisting and dispersing

the rain-drenched
cloudberries
taste of earth
and cloud

forms of availability
detachment lightness
transparency
bring the gift of the modes
of sympathy
to be able to wait
to move without obstruction
to see far

on crags and slopes
at altitude
on unstable soil
the alpine gentian
gentiana novalis
rare and local

from the crag of the stranger
grey screes fall sheer
to the green lochan
a level of pure
scree-filtered water

fallen from a height
a boulder retains
mass weight position dignity
or acquires them
in its fallen state

leeches in the shallows
of the green lochan
wait to latch on to
a passing affection
black leeches

light grey and deep grey
threaten and lure
soft grey builds distances
in finer shades of grey
cross-hatchings and scumbles
dark grey passes over

looking through greys
to blue and green
the intervening tones
give focus

rain is falling
there and here
on an earth
or ground
repeatedly affirmed
as if it were
unbelievable

too impetuous to be
anywhere
the burn rushes through
the sounds
it throws
in the air

stand sideways to the wind
or hunkering down
present the least
surface to the rain
sit it out or go on
in weather be there
or disappear

the sun comes out
and the sky clears
as decisively as if
a word had been spoken
to launch the great
cattle raid on perception

after a long walk in
to step up to the sky
is exhilarating
if only for
a moment by the cairn
before heading down

on a mountain top
the world spins
when it slows
to a stop
it leans

when the wind drops
calm is free
of predicates
a thorn
stripped of blossom

little crystals
in the ear
adjust to
pressure
as the earth tilts
over

at its upper limit
the mountain pansy
viola lutea
rooted in uncertainty
is blue and yellow
briefly

to remember it
is to visit it
again in thought
to lean
closer in
briefly

glamour stands scrutiny
the world is sonorous
spacious and chromatic
fragrant, formidable
responding to the touch

lie back in the heather
the winds are silk
cloths drawn lightly
over the slopes
the cheek bones

a basket woven
with goldenrod
and marjoram
heavy with apples
is not more welcome
than a glen that sweeps
up nothing in its arms
to offer it
for delectation

whatever is touched
steps back
the impossible flower
the immediate
at arm's length
under the fingertips

many discursive influences
pour into the argument
of a mountain burn
in a pedantry that runs on
while sense traverses it
delight rushes through it

in the din of the waterfall
overtones of bells
in the wind, variation
thrushes tapping shells
hebridean bees
listening beyond themselves
approach quiet by degrees

from turbulence to turbulence
the water fills
a hollow that holds it
still for a while
a turbulence interrupted
the stillness a constant
exchange of water

sylphs and nymphs and kelpies
might slip between
silks and shocks and sulks
of water into real bodies

consonants with varied
points of articulation
palatalised and rounded
sibilants affricates
clicks clacks diphthongs
a burn or babble
of open vowels

roots rocks boulders
stops and labials
gutters and runnels
dentals constrictives

forgetting brings loss
of articulation
the language of the heart
a smoke

stone dressed in water
a smooth or slick
drape of water
moulding its facets

the force
of water stuns
deaf to sense
things stand
astonished

there is a place
of sunlight
under birch trees
separate
across a torrent

lean closer
to the slope
inside
an antique
music trickles
it tickles
the curiosity
of the unwary

older than looking
this listening
older than listening
this lonesome
touch

efficacious songs are never sung
aloud but only under
a splashing of rushing water
aside or athwart
to the silverweed
to primrose to pearlwort

a song of herding
a song of milking
a song of smooring
a song of kindling
words on the breaking
of bread

while water flows
a tune runs contrary
tug of desire
against contingency
that it all stay
nothing be lost
the turbulence least

in an anonymous place
of couch grass and thorns
there is a parting
a lesion
something is given
into the world's keeping

sometimes a name
will be enough to loosen
desire for a while
loch of the stepping stones
no need to go there

everyone
gets soaked
to the skin
except the thin
theorist of rain

sketch of a wild rose
in watercolour
dissolving

a path laid down
in granite
leads up through
the immediate
a green of young
birch leaves
aspen leaves
trembling

on the slope, a wood
of birch and hazel
waking to morning
falls through the light
that falls through it

at an angle of light
the leaves of wild garlic
have a silver sheen
that empties their form
nowhere spreading everywhere
under the trees

as a swarm of wasps
is drawn to a slick
of aphids along
a pine branch
a quality of darkness
under the pines
is attractive

shades of green
lead farther in
to a green that glows
internally
then paths of green
close up again
behind one who passes
lightly

solitaries in community
the pines
at dawn and at dusk
in observance

all the water pouring
over the waterfall
confirms the notion
of a waterfall
the form rests
while the water flows

intelligence nimble
fine webs thrown
across branches
inference over gaps
a squirrel laughs
from high in the tree
at water falling
continually

the path picks up
again on the other
side of a fallen tree
but the intervening
bulk of the trunk
shatters complacency

the broken giants
battered foliage
jagged edges
of the great
raised wounds

to move among
crashing pines
is spacious
and exact

gear and tackle
grapple with lengths
of felled pine
the staggering
tilting weights
set down

it takes a lot
of noise to clear
old sunlight
from pine woods

the ground is a scrub
a complex weaving
or layering of bracken
bilberry and least willow
each step must be
tested carefully
a way found by forsaking
the forgetting of trust

amid storm damage
a debris of quiet
the attacked heart healing
picnic on a log

a pact for peace
a league for peace
a treaty or entreaty
for perpetual peace
a forest
for

light that might
spread indefinitely
never to be known
is trapped in leaves
and pulled down
through the tree canopy
around everybody

layers of branches
ranks of tall grasses
deposits of leaves
turf and mulch
insist on the hatching
of horizontal with vertical
as rich exchange
a constantly occurring
ascending and descending

a wind blown cloud
deepens the shade
or lightens it
by dispersing again
putting in question
the provenance of shade
its stability and spread

in a context of green
the graces dance
in weeds of green
neatly
away from inspection

toys and trinkets
placed in a tree
in recognition
of a mystery
dispersed in
toys and trinkets

one in constant
modulation
may be a tree
a bird a stone
startled
in the light
of recognition

or
the golden word
ripple of variation
lever of possibility
an oar

stone into gold
gold into stone
wheat into bread
desire to fruition
gravity to levity
dependency to autonomy
sorrow into yarrow
water into melody

year after year
it builds its nest
of twigs and grass
mud and moss
where anyone
might find it

shape shade
nuance tone
words that go in
under round
by thorn light
often torn

at a tap
a cloud
of pollen
spills
to drift
in a puff
of dust

in the light-filled wood
a wall a lintel some stairs
as if the parings of a life
were preserved in honey jars

something discrete
is led to
discretion
as if taken
by the hand

in the wood in the fall
in the woolly heads
of willow herb
a chapel in ruins

when the light shifts
countless trembling
raindrops on birch twigs
fade to a clarity that seems
the temper of the day
until light returns
to the shining tree

when a breeze blows
through grasses or branches
light touches the harp
there are no witnesses
only musicians, dancers

yellow in shade
is a modified green
cool and contained
not seeking the light
but allowing a dappled
light to find it

at the edge of shadow
a drift of speedwell
makes a pool of blue
a transition to brightness
casting retrospective
haze over shadows

if the light of the sun
is focused through a lens
it will burn
intently
giving off smoke
leaving a dark
mark of intention
sunlight on wood

after rain
briar leaves
have a scent
of apples

starting over there
and coming back
all the way across
intervening distance
where might
enquiry end

springs and wells are doors
doors are springs and wells

here is a garden
of tansy run riot
around anyone
bright enough
to neglect it

the lintel is broken
four walls still stand
sheep occupy an absence
of the well–spoken
habit of the house

nothing hides
in the abandoned places
no household gods
no folded spaces
flint left in the wall
long idle

three milking cows
tethered in the byre
hens in and out
at the scullery window
bread and cream
blue and white ware
eggs in the straw
the clock ticking

in a back parlour
the best furniture
is seldom used
linen is folded
neatly in a drawer
fresh for an occasion
that never arrives
the clock ticking

a jug of water
a chink of light
a twist of smoke

step closer
someone is there
in the shadows
looking out

by a window
blue cornflowers
in a yellow cup
continually
wake up

cleanse and thicken the cloth
by beating after weaving
rhythmically beating and singing
cleanse and thicken and soften the cloth
by soaking it and thumping it
in company in time
waulking the newly woven cloth

wash it in the burn
dry it on a thorn
sew it with a needle
with pure white thread
putting the iron on it
press it and warm it
place it crisp and folded
in the right hands

the wells and the burns
the fruits of labour
the moor and the machair
the stories and tunes
a quality of welcome
the spaces of custom
of communal negotiation
brought under authority
of gentry and clergy

rent is in kind
oats barley
wethers chickens
with a right to gather
wind scattered wits
heather and peat
on the heart slope
in the rain

before darkening
the threshold
be sure to bring
straws of brightness
shards of cold air
into company

or bring nothing
on a visit
nothing to divert
the gasp
of welcome

the crofter a weaver
the postman a baker
the fisherman a shepherd
the poet a mender of roads

a stone picked up
a weight set down
a role assumed
or discarded

neighbours on the doorstep
nomads at a border

twisting heather twigs
twining quicken roots
plaiting bentgrass
in peat reek
spinning and carding
scolding and teasing
knitting and darning
out of the sleet

bending down
by the burn
to pick fresh
water mint
did they pause
for a moment
out of the wind

woven with hazel and willow
with hazel and willow woven
woven with hazel and willow
with hazel and willow woven
woven with hazel and willow

let this
trouble pass
to a trick
or a turn
at a word
let it swerve
past

hold the bucket
under water until
the bucket fills up
then carry the bucket
up the slope careful
not to spill a drop

forgetting is a second clearance
attention to distance
loss of the near at hand

what will become of us
here on the edge
in the bitter wind
on acid soil
beside the waiting
transports

there were bridles of grasses
pulled from the machair
on the gentle horses
riding into war

a basket left
among the grasses
is soon claimed
by the grasses

how lovely now
is the fluttering
of a yellow butterfly
in the margins
of my book

warmth from the straw
draws the dew
into a hollow lined
with straw and clay
worked into a puddle
trampled by cattle
it will hold water
a cool place at noon
the dew pond

in mist filled hollows
gravity extracts
moisture from air
in the cloud pond
the fog pond
the frog pond
the dew pond

tall blind grasses
ripple in a breeze
that breathes through them
a hand brushes over them
the many-coloured grasses
knowing nothing of colour
seed in a haze
nothing rooted sees

to come down
to the shelter
of a sunlit hollow
is to step
into a warmth
of reception

nothing is deeper
than a surface of water
sipped by swallows
the slight
truth of shallows
support of lilies

across the level
expanse of the lochan
point instants of rain
hardly remain
for long enough
to register
here and there
there and here

flowers rare
leaves light green
floating on water
lemna minor
small green ovals
drifting in shoals
in ditches and pools

the negative space
of the lochan
replaces earth with sky
a gap in pure extension
it is an overturning
of the reasonable
the dry

when ducks push through
duckweed it floats
in again behind them

on the fiddler's path
along the river
notes play over
notes of water
in a continuous stream of sound
the waulking of the plaiding
daft robin
a slow air

thrushes take the tune
and all the family
of hedges and distances
answer in antiphony

the blackbird in the hedge
warbler on a thorn
thrush of the afternoon
sweeter their notes than bells
harps or accordions

aside from the path
the anti-fiddler
scrapes away
at nothing
picking and unpicking
the plaid of sense
in a farewell to whisky
a slow air

sanding it down
paring it down
the rind
the integument
diluting it
thinning it
the defining line
the boundary

in the heat of afternoon
quiet suffers reduction
to a one stone drone
a latent power
dangerous to strangers

if shade were shelter
for things from their names
the young bull might sit
in imageless absorption
its ferocity cooling

willow branches lift and fall
and in falling seem to slow
to lag behind an inference
of the course of respiring branches
an image settling like snow

the hill that was dark
is now bright
imperceptibly sensation
glows to emotion
then fades again

it flaps away
the lapwing
it claps away
laps away
away

the scent of meadowsweet
a memory of the scent
of meadowsweet

impetuous
little flurry
of raindrops
on the brushed
snare drum
of the pond

to go on and on
to have more of the same
is the one desire
of the solitary walker
in the just intonation
of the river meadow
in late afternoon

arcs and loops and angles
long leisurely
flights of abstraction
of lines over water
settle on water
sedge on the evening rise

the land of twilight
of the sunset
the west
a land of evening
of a levelling
prolonged

the weaving of grasses dust
dust the weaver of grasses

far out on the lochan
two red-throated divers
drift on the water
this way and that
in a lack of volition
given to the water
turning together
this way and that

if you were mine
I would hold you
if you were mine
I would rock you
if you were mine
I would lift you
over the stile
into morning

little muntjack deer
running through the corn
in flight from form
in the gloaming

preserve us from calm
that brings in the night
harm to islands

a lamp of fish oil
with a wick of rushes
gathered by the light
of the full moon